What Is This?

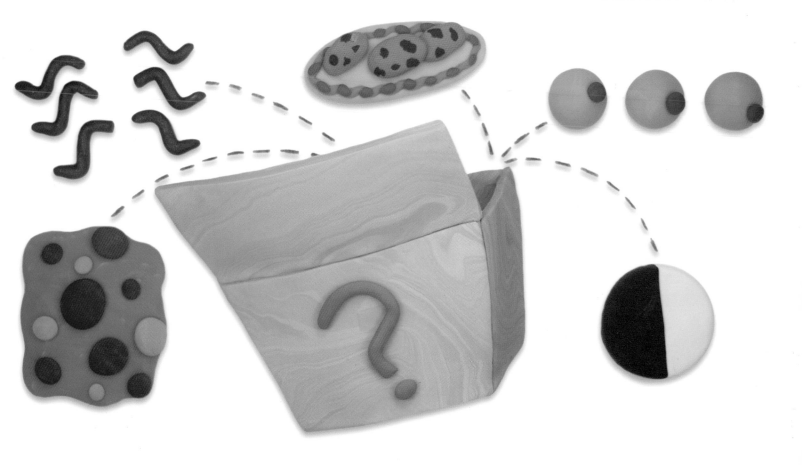

It is green.

It has two eyes.

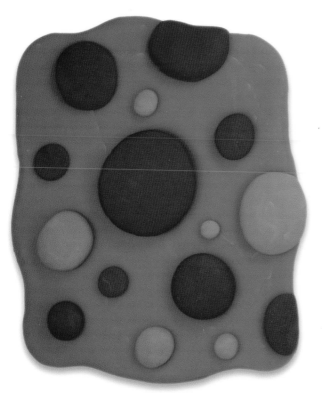

It has spots.

It can hop.

What is this?

3

This is a frog.

This has eight legs. It likes bugs.

It is on a web. What is this?

It is a spider.

It is black and white.　　　It is round.

I can kick it. What is this?

This is a soccer ball.

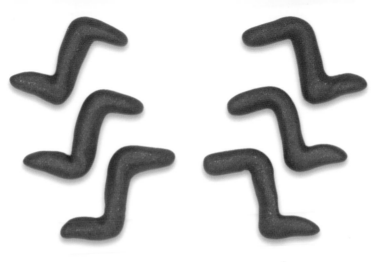

This has six legs.

It likes cookies. What is this?

It is an ant.

This likes milk.

It is my pet.

What is this?

This is my cat.

This is round.
It can be all colors.

It has a stick.

What is this?

This is a lollipop. Yum!

This is orange and purple.

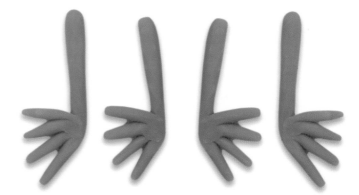

It has three eyes.   **It has four legs.**

What is this?

This is my monster!